Lizzie
Mary
Cullen

The
Magical

A
Colouring
Book

City

PENGUIN BOOKS

PENGUIN BOOKS

UK | USA | Canada | Ireland | Australia
India | New Zealand | South Africa

Penguin Books is part of the Penguin Random House group of companies
whose addresses can be found at global.penguinrandomhouse.com.

Penguin
Random House
UK

First published 2015
005

Designed by Couper Street Type Co.
Printed and bound in Italy by Printer Trento S.R.L.

A CIP catalogue record for this book is available from the British Library

ISBN: 978-1-405-92409-2

www.greenpenguin.co.uk

This is a book for anyone who wishes to look beyond
the grey city and see the true magic and grace of our world.

Behind every dark building, across each muddy river,
there is gentle beauty.

Stop and breathe. See the birds in the sky.
Savour the scent of the air. In being present, even the
darkest of cities can shine with the pure and
simple joy of being alive.

In these pages you'll find different spaces, different
places. They're yours now. Enjoy them, love them
and bring their magic into your world.

Exploring the Magical City

Before you get started, turn to page 88 for a tester page so that you can try out your colouring materials on this paper. Then you're ready to enjoy this book as you wish ... colour, doodle and let your imagination run free.

And as you explore these cities, you'll see that there's much more than immediately meets the eye. You'll find reminders that we share our urban surroundings with wildlife, hidden in the illustrations ...

See how many of these you can find.

A fox

A cat

A crab

A possum

A seal

A panda

Two rats

Two lions

Two kangaroos

Three dragons

Eighteen birds

Twenty-two fishes

Or, if they're being too elusive,
turn to page 90 for the answers.

London Panorama

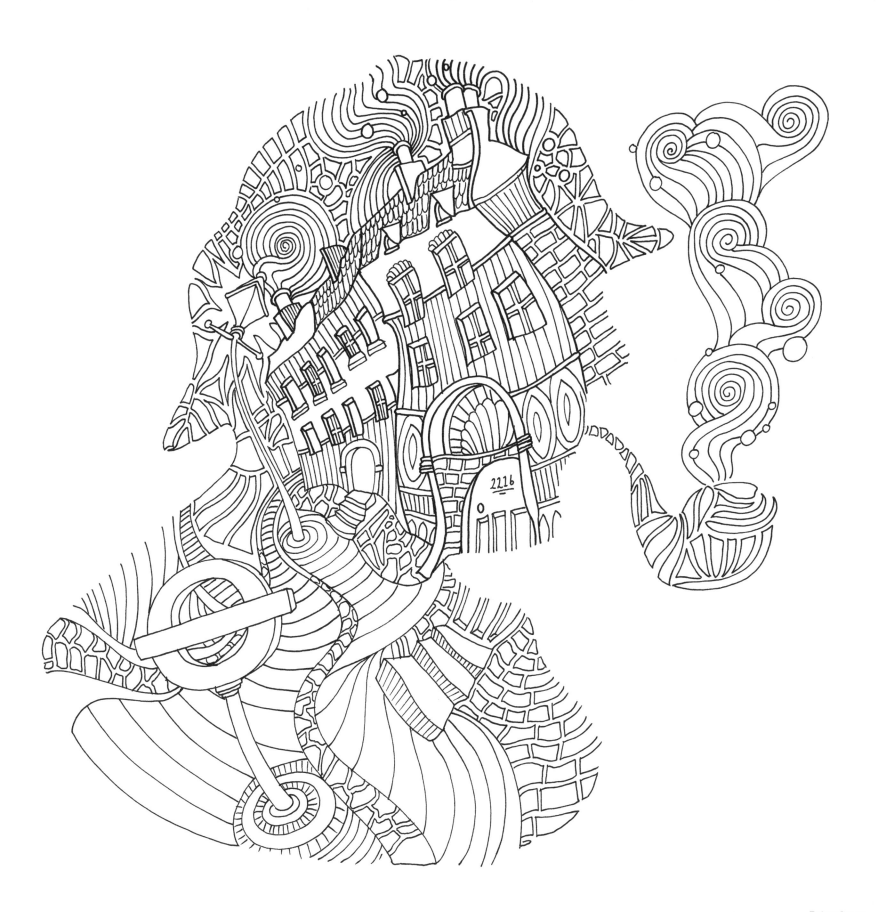

Baker Street

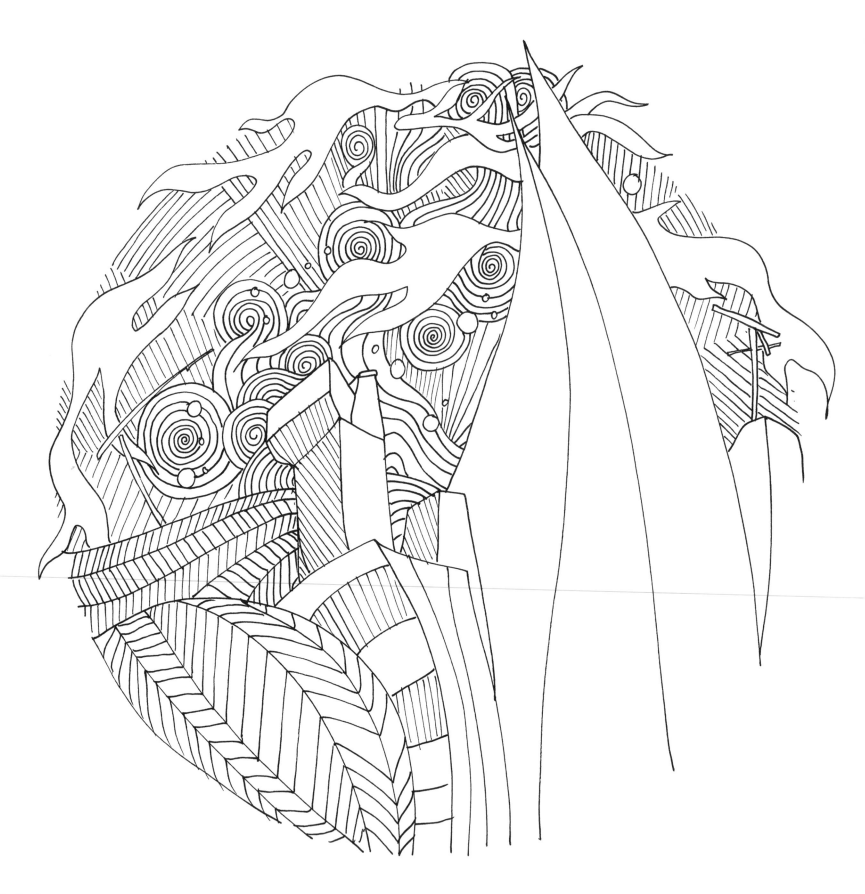

The Shard

Piccadilly Circus

Chimneys
and Rooftops

Bruges

The Great Wall of China

Mount Fuji

Luxor

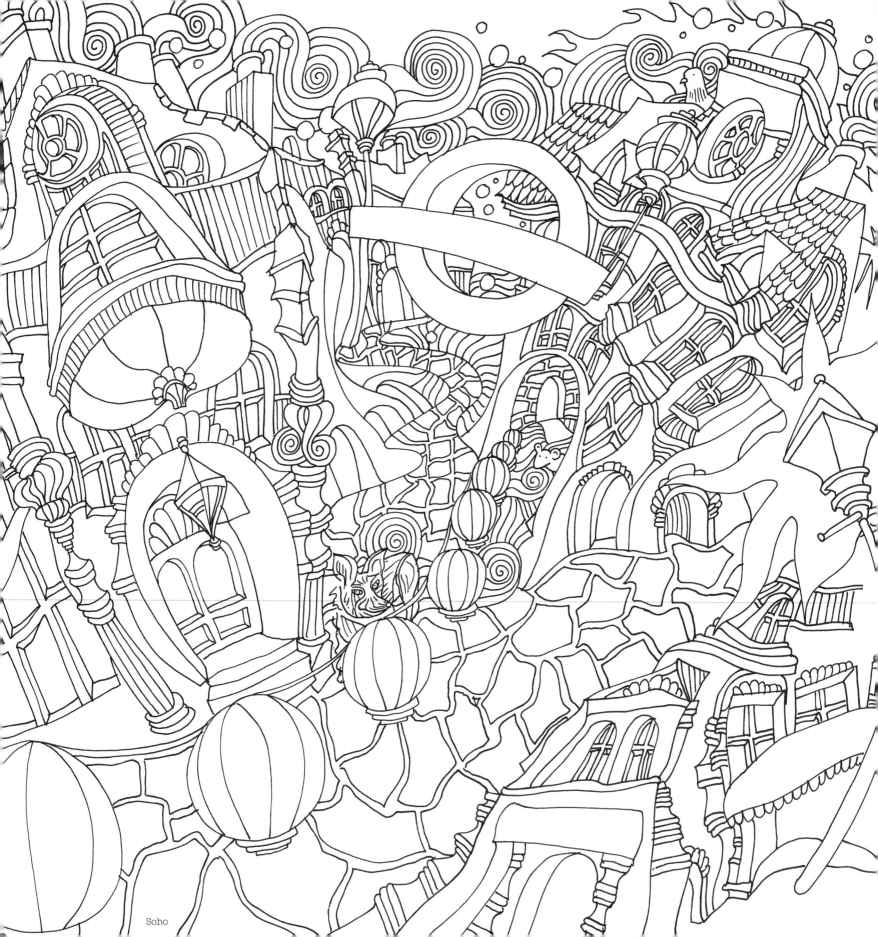

Soho

Coverack

Old English Village

Little Moreton Hall

Eiffel Tower

Paris

Tate Britain

The Globe

Stained Glass

Bridge through Town

Moulin Rouge

Paris

Paris

Goldsmiths

Tower Bridge

Cobbled Streets

Midnight

Tokyo

Charlottenburg Palace, Berlin

EST. 1887

ALICES

ANTIQUES

PORTOBELLO ROAD W.11

Portobello Road

San Francisco

Seattle

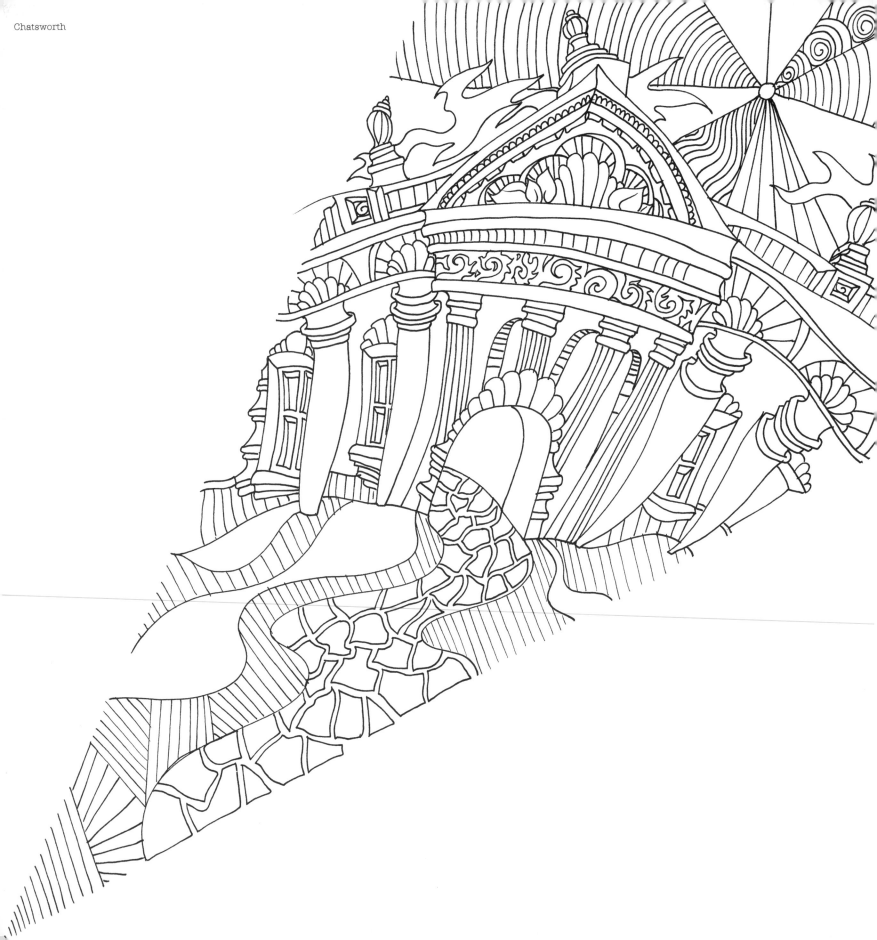

St Pancras

Chinese Palace

Northern Lights

Barcelona

The Colosseum

Sydney

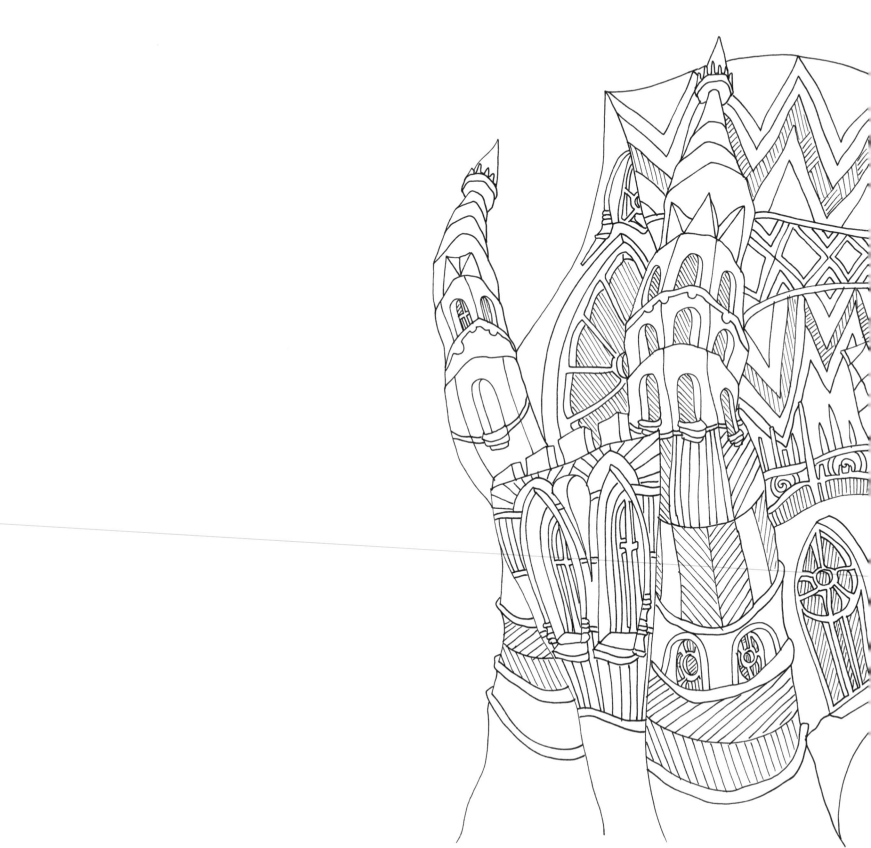

Stephen's Dome, Vienna

Stockholm

Venice

Waterfall

Archway

Abbey Road

Chester

Medieval City

Red House, Bexleyheath

New York

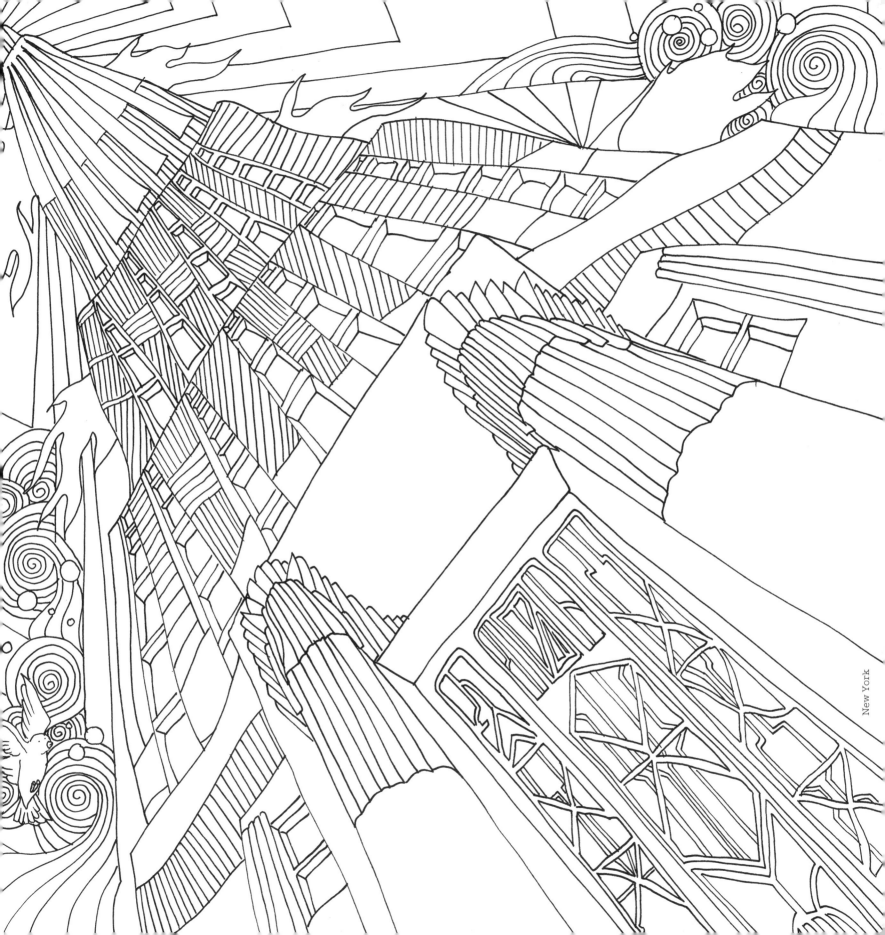

New York

Ronda, Spain

Malta

Carcassonne, France

Castle on the Hill

Medieval Castle

Staircases

Moscow

St Basil's Cathedral

Ischia, Italy

Jardin Majorelle, Marrakech

Edinburgh

Newcastle

Amsterdam

Rio de Janeiro

Taj Mahal

Test Page

Try out your colouring materials on this practice image.

Acknowledgements

There are many people that I'd like to thank who have helped me develop and grow over the years. I've gone down the rabbit hole exploring the sometimes-mysterious world of psychogeography. Exploring, mapping, discovering, and seeing new spaces. It's brought me so much joy, and led me down a fascinating path.

I wouldn't have found this special world without my time on the Goldsmiths design BA course. Thank you to Rosario Hurtado for always expecting more, and asking 'why?'. To Matt Ward for identifying that my scribbles were my first steps to developing my own psychogeographic mapping process, and to Belinda Magee for her endless support and kind guidance.

A big thank you to Louisa and the New Designers team for giving me the opportunity to showcase my graduate work. At the show I had the great fortune to meet Pia Fairhurst who gave me my first big commission. A huge thank you for the incredible gift of four years of work creating murals for Zizzi restaurants across the country. At the New Designers show I also crossed paths with Lynda Relph-Knight who has been an endless source of support and has become a dear friend.

To Ray and Irena at Artefact Picture Framers and The Framers Gallery who have supported me from the beginning. To every person and company who has ever used my work – thank you for helping me grow as an artist and an illustrator. To Bradley Garrett for letting me share your adventures. To Serena Morton for having faith in me. And huge gratitude to the continuing support of the Association of Illustrators who constantly fight for fair wages for illustrators and artists across the UK and abroad.

A profound thank you to the Beehive Design Collective in Machias, Maine, for welcoming me into your world. To Sofia and Pam for igniting something new and beautiful in my soul. To Lesley, Freda and the tribe, thank you for our beautiful White Pine Day, and embracing us into your family. And thank you to the bear on the abandoned railway line for not eating me.

To the crew at Penguin – thank you to Fenella Bates, Fiona Crosby and the team for giving me this wonderful opportunity. Thank you to my agent Chris Wellbelove for kicking this project into life. And to Lizzie for introducing us.

Thank you to all my dear dear friends. You know who you are. My little world would be far less beautiful without you. To my grandparents, Rosie and Roo, for their kind, brave hearts. And to Rachel, Ed, Tom, the Parkhouses, the Brothers and the Cullens, for all your love and care.

And finally, to Mum and Dad – thank you for everything. I love you.

Key to the Magical City

2 Pigeons

Camden

Baker Street

1 Dragon

The Shard

Piccadilly Circus

Chimney's and Rooftops

Bruges

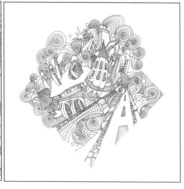

The Great Wall of China

1 Giant Panda

90

Mount Fuji

Luxor

1 Mandarin Duck

1 Falcon, 1 Heron

Soho

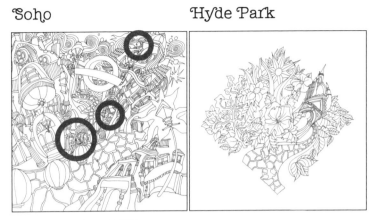

Hyde Park

1 Fox, 1 Rat, 1 Pigeon

Coverack

Old English Village

1 Cornish Seal

Little Moreton Hall

3 Perch, 2 Hawks

Eiffel Tower

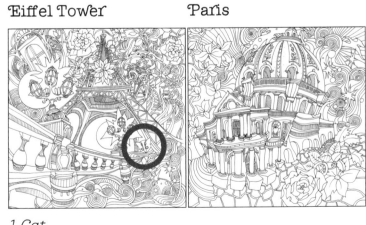

Paris

1 Cat

Tate Britain

The Globe

2 Lions

Stained Glass

Bridge through Town

Moulin Rouge

Paris

Paris

Goldsmiths

Tower Bridge

Cobbled Streets

Midnight

Tokyo

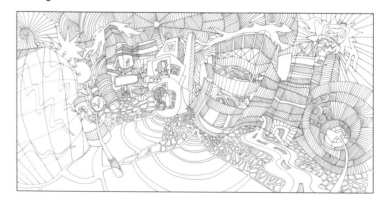

Charlottenburg Palace, Berlin

Portobello Road

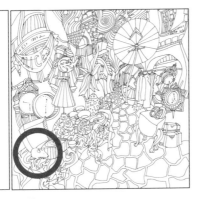

1 Rat

San Francisco

Seattle

1 Virginia Possum

Chatsworth

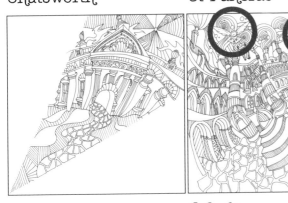

St Pancras

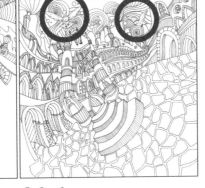

2 Owls

Chinese Palace

2 Dragons

International Space Station

Northern Lights

Barcelona

The Colosseum

Sydney

Memphis

Stephen's Dome, Vienna

2 Kangaroos

Stockholm

Venice

1 Pigeon, 3 Dusky Groupers

Waterfall

Archway

Abbey Road

Tower of London

Chester

Medieval City

Red House,
Bexleyheath

New York

New York

2 Swallows

1 Eastern Bluebird

Ronda, Spain

Malta

Carcassonne, France

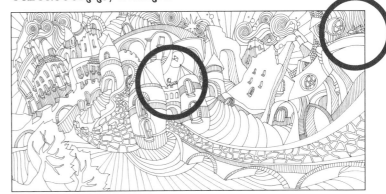

2 Woodchat Shrikes

Castle on the Hill

Medieval Castle

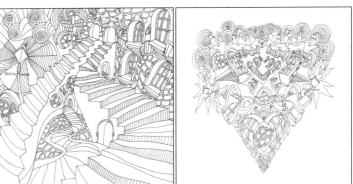

Staircases

City Mirror

Moscow

St Basil's Cathedral

Ischia, Italy

1 Crab, 15 Brown Trout

Jardin Majorelle, Marrakech

Edinburgh

Newcastle

Amsterdam

Rio de Janeiro

1 Red-Necked Tanager

Taj Mahal

1 Indian Roller